TO CATCH MY
BREATH

A STORY OF LOVE, FAITH, AND SURVIVING A DOUBLE LUNG TRANSPLANT

BUDDY NORRIS

with Amy Norris

HIGH BRIDGE BOOKS
HOUSTON

To Catch My Breath
by Buddy Norris

Printed in the United States of America
ISBN: 978-1-954943-47-6

High Bridge Books titles may be purchased in bulk for educational, business, fundraising, or sales promotional use. For information, please contact High Bridge Books via www.HighBridgeBooks.com/contact.

Published in Houston, Texas by High Bridge Books

Cover photography by Dianne Tripp.
Taken at Shallotte Riverwalk in Shallotte, NC

Black & white photos by Amy C. Norris

Special thanks to Amy Norris, who took most of the black-and-white photos reprinted in this book. Amy carefully documented our entire transplant journey through her candid photography. If not for her foresight and willingness to capture images of our most disturbing moments, many treasured memories would have been lost. I thank God for Amy, not only because of her tender strength as my wife and caregiver but also because she recorded God's faithfulness to us through still photography.

Thanks Mr. Bill Vick!

We'd like to dedicate this book
to our good friend & fellow IPF warrior himself
Mr. Bill Vick,
founder of IPF Warriors, and for his
never-ending fight to cure IPF

Contents

1

The Flight to Atlanta

November 24, 2014

I WASN'T STRONG ENOUGH to step up onto the wing of the small airplane from Angel Flight. Only about two feet separated the wing from the ground. A matter of one step and I'd be on the wing. Then I could slide across it and fall into the cockpit if I had to. In my condition, though, those two feet might as well have been a climb up Mt. Everest. I couldn't lift my foot, but I couldn't just leave it on the ground either. I was running out of time, and Amy and I both knew it.

Two people I had not noticed before came up behind me to help. With one person supporting each arm, these two helpers boosted me high enough to get my foot onto the narrow wing of the plane. It didn't help. I lacked even the strength to push up the weight of my own body, now almost 60 pounds lighter than it was a few months earlier. My angel-helpers lifted me again, this time giving me just enough momentum to land facedown on the small, shiny wing. Now I was on my own. It was up to me to get to the cockpit door. So weak I couldn't stand on my own power, I didn't have the energy to pull myself in the door of the plane using the overhead hand grip. Dragging an oxygen tank behind me didn't help anything.

For nearly two years, I'd been confined to a wheelchair and on oxygen 24/7. Although I forced myself to exercise daily by walking on the treadmill near my bed, I was still severely deconditioned. To survive, I needed a double lung transplant. Five times I'd been rejected for a transplant. Five times I'd been told to go home, call hospice, and enjoy what time I had left with my family and friends. And five times, Amy and I had refused to quit.

Three rejections came from Duke alone, one from Pittsburgh, and one from the Cleveland Clinic. Funny that Pittsburgh and Cleveland turned me down sight unseen. They never so much as took my temperature. Their rejections were based solely on Duke's findings that were included in my medical records. Those records were sent ahead of me every time I applied somewhere else. I soon figured that out and stopped all my medical records from being forwarded ahead of me. Instead, I showed up with only what I absolutely had to have in a file. That way, the medical team members would have to form their own opinions based on their evaluations and findings. It worked! I got in the door with at least one chance at life at Emory University Hospital in Atlanta, Georgia. Before that, I was just a sitting duck with no chance whatsoever.

Today my new lungs were waiting 359 miles away. I was either getting on this plane tonight or getting measured for a coffin tomorrow. There were no other options at this point. By God's hand, I slid to the door and then inside the plane. I barely remember getting into my seat. It didn't matter to me if I was upside down in my seat; if I was on board, that's all that mattered. My wife buckled in behind me. This flight would carry us to my last chance at new lungs—really, my last chance at life. I only had days to live without a transplant, and I knew I'd never be able to do another six-minute walk or anything else required. I was too weak now. One way or another, this was it. A strange peace fell over me. I was relieved to know that my struggle to live would soon be over. I'd either be healed while still here on earth or healed in heaven with a brand new, heavenly body. Right now, I simply wanted air. I was desperate to breathe.

Our plane departed from Myrtle Beach, SC, around 6:00 p.m. on November 24, 2014. I looked out the window. Darkness was already falling. As we climbed higher, the weather turned worse. Lightning flashed outside, and thunder shook our small aircraft. I couldn't see anything but darkness ahead and the lights of the cities below as the pilot, Amy, and I passed over them.

None of us had uttered even one word since the pilot introduced himself. We were all in deep thought, focused on getting to Atlanta alive. The pilot spoke to someone on his radio about how bad the weather had gotten. He told them he was going to try to climb above the storm. That sounded good to me. How ironic would it be to die in a plane crash on the way to the transplant that was supposed to save my life? The pilot made one more transmission over the radio before tilting the plane's nose upward, searching for space above the storm. Silence descended again in the cockpit and stayed with us for the remainder of the two-hour flight.

My wife gently patted my shoulder. I felt her touch, as reassuring as her voice, say, "It's all right, Buddy. It's all going to be just fine." But I wasn't confident that anything would be just fine. Would it really be alright? My breathing had grown so labored that I wondered if it was already too late for me. I rubbed the cross pendant that had hung around my neck from the beginning of this journey and prayed like Amy and I had done so many times before. Prayer had gotten us this far, and I was confident it would continue to do so because God was still with us.

2

The Diagnosis

December 30, 2009

I ARRIVED 10 MINUTES early for my annual eye exam.

Everything appeared to be checking out fine until the last test. I heard the optician say "hmmm" while looking into my left eye with a bright light. Hmmm is never something I want to hear from any doctor at any exam. I didn't hear any real concern in her voice, so I didn't let that make me nervous, just a little curious. Besides, I had other things on my mind that day.

"Is everything okay?" I asked her.

"The optic nerve in your left eye has a spot on it," she said, switching off her light.

"What does that mean?" I asked.

"It might not be anything at all, but this is something we sometimes observe in people with cystic fibrosis," she replied. "Come back tomorrow and we'll redo the test just to see if it's still there."

The next day, the spot was still there. The optician recommended I see a specialist. One CT scan and one lung biopsy later, a pulmonologist finally confirmed that I did not have cystic fibrosis.

"Okay then," I said. "Great news! So it's nothing, right?" "Buddy," the pulmonologist said, "you've tested positive for idiopathic pulmonary fibrosis."

I knew nothing about that diagnosis and less about its treatment. I'd never even heard of it. I asked him the most logical questions I could think of: "A pill should take care of it, right? An antibiotic maybe?"

"There's always a double lung transplant," he said.

"Come on, doc. A double lung transplant?"

But I felt fine. I didn't have any problems with my lungs at all. Not a single symptom of lung disease. Surely there was an easier way to treat this than a transplant. So Amy and I left the pulmonologist's office. Somewhere in the parking lot on our way to the car, it hit me, the magnitude of what the pulmonologist had just told us. I stopped and looked at Amy and said, "I'm dying. I'm really dying."

Amy replied, "There's no way I'm going to be a widow in three to five years."

That was the timeframe the pulmonologist had told us was the life expectancy of someone with IPF. I don't think a word was spoken the entire ride back home that day.

Once at home, we started piecing together what we knew to see how we'd found ourselves with this diagnosis. Earlier that fall, Amy remembered, we'd decided to play a little tennis one day. After 15 minutes, I felt winded and left the court. At the time, we put it down to me being me— overweight and still smoking. Still, it had never been a problem before.

The Diagnosis

The truth began to sink in. What caused my breathlessness was neither my weight nor my cigarette habit. It had a name—this monster had a name, and it was called idiopathic pulmonary fibrosis (IPF). Idiopathic means "no identifiable cause." Pulmonary means "related to the lungs." Fibrosis refers to the thickening and scarring of connective tissue. My lungs were stiffening. Where all those tiny cells should flex, allowing air in and out of my body, there would soon be rigid scar tissue. Normal lungs inflate like a latex balloon. Soon they would be about as flexible as a leather football. No one could tell me why this was happening, but it wasn't just going to go away.

I was dying. Why else would I need something as serious as a complete double lung transplant if I weren't dying? Over the years, I'd heard other people pray those desperate prayers to God. I'd been a born-again Christian for almost all my life, and I wasn't impressed with people turning to God only when they needed something. That wasn't for me, although I sometimes fell into that same category at desperate times. Amy and I had always prayed for what we needed. Sometimes we just thanked God for all He had done in our lives. Other times, we prayed for other people's needs. But sure enough, let a crisis hit us, and here we were, begging God to save us as if we were people drowning in a shipwreck. I felt ashamed to ask God for anything for myself.

I was raised by Christian parents. My father was a pastor. Mom played the organ and taught youth Sunday school. Both my younger sisters were active Christians. I'd tried to live my life as a Christian too, but I'd fallen short so many times in my past, dabbling in drugs and alcohol. But He's a God of love and forgiveness. He said there was no limit to how many times He'd forgive us and cast our sins as far as the east is from the west. For that reason, I knew I could ask him for anything and I'd still be worthy to receive it. It did not, however, mean He would give it to me. God knows what we need better than we do. Sometimes our greatest gifts and blessings come in the form of unanswered prayers. So Amy and I put it all in His hands, asking Him to do as He saw fit and in accordance with His plans for each of us.

3

A Rapid Decline

MY IPF DIAGNOSIS LAUNCHED more than a physical battle for my life. It also forged an intimate relationship with God like I had never known before. I found myself mostly alone in my quiet bedroom for hours upon hours daily, and weeks sometimes. At the time, I was unable to walk much or get around very well, but I could pray and just talk to God like a friend. So that's what I did day in and day out. I talked and I listened, and I read the Word, my Bible.

God and I became close. He gave me a supernatural spiritual understanding, awareness, and sensitivity to Him, His love, and His presence that I never knew even existed until then. At times He was almost visible to me, sitting with me in my bedroom by the bed, holding my hand and telling me in an audible voice that everything would be alright. Sometimes it made me feel like I would meet Him soon and that this was only part of the transition from life to death. If that was so, I wasn't as excited about meeting God like I thought a Christian should be.

I was naturally scared of dying in my physical existence just the same. There's an instinct to live that takes over the mind and the body when death is close. I believed this now more than ever, and I believed that was what I was experiencing along with this newfound spiritual awareness of mine. Or maybe … maybe God meant He was going to heal me here on this earth and give me more years with my family and friends here. I just didn't know.

Early on, I had no obvious physical symptoms—no coughing, no shortness of breath, nothing. At times, I doubted that I was even as sick as the doctors were telling me I was. I had even more doubt that I was dying … but I was. Things progressed. I found that the drive alone to my pulmonologist's office, only 25 minutes away, was getting to be harder for me. The thought of changing to one closer to home seemed crazy though. But then, in early 2012, I did it anyway and found a different pulmonologist just 10 minutes from my house, and it seemed to be the right thing to do at that time. It sure was easier in my condition. That would turn out to be a huge mistake.

In the summer of 2012, I found I couldn't go to the beach and walk from the parking lot to the strand anymore like I always had before. Now, Amy would drop me off at the beach access with all the chairs, towels, and snacks in the cooler for our day at the beach. Then she'd park the car and walk back to where I was still waiting. Amy would carry everything down on the strand by herself, bless her heart. I still had to walk to where she would put the chairs as close to the parking lot as possible to make for a shorter walk back for me later. It was all I could do, and that just barely, but I wanted to go because the ocean breeze was healing for me. It would take what felt like forever to recover and catch my breath again after I finally got to and sat down in my beach chair.

When we left, I had to repeat the short walk back to the highway, where Amy would pick me up and we'd head home. The coughing attack I always had when I got back in the car was unforgiving. The heat had weakened me even more, and the transition from the hot air outside to the AC in the car had a negative effect on me and would cause awful coughing spells every time.

By the following summer, it just wasn't possible for me to even walk from the beach access to the strand anymore without becoming severely winded. For this veteran surfer of 20+ years, that was a tough thing to accept. Once, I had been capable of paddling my surfboard out against stormy hurricane-force waves. Now, I could no longer even walk the short distance to the water's edge just to sit. Did I mention it was embarrassing? Did I also mention it was humbling? Did I mention that God knew what He was doing in me? Well, He did. He was breaking me to bring me closer to Him—to make me flexible so that He could work on me. He was putting me in a position where I had nobody but Him to turn to. I wasn't as close to Him as I needed to be— or as I used to be. But we were growing close again. My beach days were pretty much over except for the occasional, rare morning when I was able to walk on the beach. Walking was—and still is—very important.

4

Tested on Every Side (But Not in Despair)

EVERY WEEK THE DREADED oxygen order was submitted for home delivery. It wasn't unusual to see up to 30 to 35 E-cylinder oxygen tanks on our back porch at any given time. I had been experiencing shortness of breath, and at times, my oxygen level dropped well below acceptable limits. Ideally, oxygen levels run north of 95%. Mine would drop into the 80s. When it didn't come back up, it was time for oxygen around the clock. I found it impossible to do anything without that oxygen cannula in my nose. At first, they only gave me small tanks, but eventually, my levels dropped so low that I needed a full-time supply of the E-cylinders and larger tanks like the M60. The doctor also prescribed prednisone and various inhalers to help keep my airways as open as possible. Still, I grew weaker and shorter of breath as the IPF progressed.

One day as I was reading my Bible, I came upon 2 Corinthians 12:10, which says, "For when I am weak, then am I strong." It hit me that the weaker my body became physically, the stronger my spirit seemed to get. This short scripture became my personal favorite from God to me, the one

I clung to throughout this painful journey. I'm not sure it was written to mean this at all, but it meant that to me and I thanked God for it.

God's presence brought comfort, but it didn't bring answers. How had I contracted IPF? I had worked in facilities with asbestos, silica, and two-part spray paint/epoxies. I'd been a carpenter for a few years and had inhaled a lot of sawdust. The possibilities were endless. Surely one of these had to be the culprit that had caused me to contract IPF. My guess was always that the damage to my lungs was easily done at a nuclear plant where I'd worked in my past. I had worked in what they called the blast yard, where I'd sandblasted and spray painted, unknowingly, without the correct safety equipment for a long time. Now I would pay the piper. And he was expensive.

My pulmonologist briefly mentioned that I would need a referral to Duke if I were going to get accepted into their transplant program. Fortunately, early in my illness, my brother-in-law Todd Morton remembered someone we'd gone to high school with who worked at Duke. I reached out to her for information, which resulted in her helping me get in to see their doctors in early 2013. It gave us a much-needed head start.

We were set—or so we thought at the time. Amy and I had it all planned out. Duke sat just three hours from our home. I had a sister who lived within an hour of the hospital. While I was recovering from my transplant, family and friends could come and go easily. Perfect scenario. So this was the place for us.

We knew we'd have to relocate and live within an hour of the hospital for a period after the transplant. Duke made sense because Amy would be able to return to work early and come up on weekends to help. A great plan, right? Maybe, but we never got to put it into action.

I soon found myself feeling uncomfortable with the pulmonary doctor I'd transferred to in early 2012. She refused to look at me and hardly even acknowledged me when we were talking during my visits. Amy was a person to her, but I was just a patient. That didn't work. Communication was very important to me, and I didn't feel like I had any with this doctor. So I found another pulmonologist. I struggled with this decision because we were three years into this battle, and I didn't know if I could safely make another change at this point. But I DID! Amy and I learned that it was necessary to have complete trust and confidence in the doctors who were guiding us through this ordeal. There would be no room for mistakes or wasted time. That's when we found Dr. Barton Schneyer, a pulmonologist, and he was amazing. We stayed with him, and he proved to be instrumental in getting me accepted for my transplant.

Finally, our appointment day arrived, and Amy and I drove to Duke University Medical Center, supposedly one of the most successful hospitals for organ transplants in the country. Duke's team would evaluate me for a double lung transplant. The trick to receiving an organ transplant, like the lungs, is that you must be sick enough to qualify for one to even be considered, yet still well enough to survive the dangerous and lengthy surgery. That leaves you with a very small window to hit just right in order to get in. But God, who can do all things, had orchestrated our transplant perfectly—as only He could.

At Duke, the medical team put me through pulmonary function tests (PFTs), chest X-rays, a six-minute walk and blood labs mostly. The first time I ever experienced a six-minute walk, I asked the tech, "Why is it called a six-minute walk?"

"Because that's what you're going to do," she told me. "You'll walk as fast as you can for six minutes.

"What are you going to do?" I asked.

"I'll walk beside you and take your oxygen saturation levels with this little O2 meter on your fingertip. This test might not seem like a big deal, but it can be the one determining factor as to whether you get a transplant or not. That test always reveals how well your lungs are working."

A six-minute walk may sound easy, but it feels like a six-mile walk when you can barely breathe from the exertion of walking across your bedroom. Just brushing my teeth would even leave me seriously winded. I had learned at an early stage in my disease that it takes oxygen to do anything and everything. Lifting my arms above my head alone had become a task. I would do the six-minute walk many more times after that initial exposure. Each time it would get harder to complete. It also grew more critical as the medical teams weighed the decision to list me for a double lung transplant.

Then came the pulmonary function tests, or PFTs. These were relentless. I had to sit in an enclosed booth with a hose in my mouth. The technician coached me to blow into it as hard as I could for as long as I could as many times as I could, while the technician took readings of my lung volume and air force. It seemed to go on forever.

Chest x-rays became the norm at every visit. All the scar tissue, which started in the lower lobes of both lungs, lit up as white patches on the x-rays. It can be confused with pneumonia and misdiagnosed, a critical mistake doctors make sometimes, but it all had to be done to measure the performance of my lungs as they declined. The tests also played a big part in the decision of whether I would or wouldn't be listed for a transplant.

5

Rejected!

IPF HAD ALREADY STARTED to turn my lungs into solid, non-functioning, and rigid scar tissue. When that scar tissue finally took over the entirety of my normal lung tissue, I would no longer be able to breathe. I knew I was racing against the clock, but I thought all I had to do was pass these tests, check into the hospital, get my transplant, stay a week or so, and then return to my life. Sounded simple enough, right? Easy. Quick. I had no idea. The adventure we were about to embark on would turn out to be many things, but not simple, easy, or quick.

As the months went by, I found it harder to do even rudimentary things. When I walked upstairs to our bedroom at night, for example, I had to make two or three stops to rest. It finally became an impossible task for me, so Amy and I were forced to move into the bedroom downstairs. The doctors told me I had to exercise every day, no matter how hard it was, to be as fit as possible just to be eligible to be listed for a transplant.

The bilateral (double) lung transplant is one of the most dangerous and lengthy surgeries there is. If a transplant came through, even if it was six months later, I had to be strong enough to survive the lengthy surgery. Exercise was a problem though. Not only was the disease sapping my strength, but for the previous two years, I had gotten very little exercise due to the limitations of my third back surgery and second neck surgery, both unrelated to IPF. With all the hardware, plates, and screws holding my vertebrae together, I was in constant pain. IPF turned pain into torture, but I pushed myself. I had no choice. And without God and without Amy's constant inspiration, I couldn't have done it even one day.

The list of things I had to do in order to save my life kept getting longer and seemed more and more impossible to achieve. Yet each one was just as important as the other, and they each demanded my full attention. Impossible right? I thought so too, but we got it done with the good Lord's help.

News had spread fast that I needed a miracle. Family, friends, and even strangers from churches and homes across the country prayed diligently for us. I had seen other devoted Christians lose their lives to this disease even after praying and believing that God would heal them. Why should my case end any differently? I wasn't anybody special to God. He loves us all the same. Sometimes God doesn't answer prayers for good reason. He sees the big picture, the big plan, and not just our personal battles sometimes. So don't get me wrong, yes, I knew God could heal me and make me whole again, but would He heal me here on earth or in heaven? God's answer—when it came—was clear.

Rejected!

I still hadn't walked my daughter down the aisle, and I wanted to meet my grandchildren. I wasn't ready to leave Amy here alone either, although I knew there was a good chance that I would. I tried not to dwell on it but to keep my mind focused on what I needed to do next and what His will was for me. To get through this battle, I could only move one step at a time. I tried to be the strongest warrior I could be.

I needed to remain mobile and keep up my strength for what was to come, so I signed up for pulmonary rehab at our local hospital. I went every day that I could. Just walking from the hospital parking lot to the rehab room took more energy and breath than I had. Thank the Lord there was a bench about halfway, where I could rest up to finish the walk, although just barely. By the time I got to the exercise room, I would be totally exhausted. So I always considered that as part of my workout too.

I still had a lot of pride though. Before IPF, I had been a strong and healthy man of 6'4", 270 pounds, so I tried to hide my weaknesses. Once inside the rehab room, I set the treadmill on very slow and concentrated on putting one foot in front of the other. I was attached to oxygen for the duration of my workout. Most days, I could manage—with God's help—to take the long walk back to the same bench in the Novant Hospital Rehab Hallway and rest for 15 to 20 minutes. Then I would slowly make my way back to my truck to drive myself back home.

Just walking in and out of rehab each day was enough exercise for me, but I pushed myself to do more when possible. From the decline I was already experiencing, I knew the time was fast approaching when I would no longer be able to get up and do any more exercise. I had to build up strength to endure a transplant now and then pray it would be enough to sustain me if the wait ran much longer. And it did—run much longer, I mean.

It seemed like an eternity before we heard back from the hospital. One day, Amy walked in with an envelope in her hand and tears in her eyes. She didn't have to say a word. Duke had denied me a transplant due to a neuromuscular problem. I felt like I had been kicked in the teeth. We hadn't prepared for or even expected this response. How would I fix this? Could I fix it? No, it was in God's hands. Only the God who made me could repair me now.

We had sunk all our time and energy into getting into only one hospital so far, Duke, because we didn't know we could apply for a transplant to more than one hospital at a time. It's called multi-listing. It's a common practice in the organ transplant world and can greatly improve your chances of being accepted by a hospital. Doctors don't usually get upset, and no one will drop you from their transplant list if you multi-list. In fact, it could be a fatal mistake if you don't. It almost was for me. We had spent a whole year trying to get into Duke alone, only to be turned down and forced to start over somewhere else. We didn't have that kind of time to waste again. And now we couldn't get it back.

Rejected!

At times, the battle for my life seemed more spiritual than physical. It branched out in many directions, each one of equal importance and each demanding our full attention and sacrifice, which was, of course, impossible. Our lives had taken an abrupt turn, and we'd been flung into a frightening medical, mental, and spiritual battle full of red tape, physical challenges, and rules we didn't understand. The list of challenges just grew and grew.

Besides all that, my increasing physical abnormalities steadily diminished my chances of being listed for a double lung transplant. My escalating weakness prompted me more and more to just quit. My body screamed out for rest—total rest, 24/7. Yet I knew that if I allowed my weakness to dictate my actions, I'd soon be bedridden. That would be a death sentence. So I pushed forward and fought with everything left in me—everything I had and all I didn't have too. God provided the rest. He was always near to me, letting me know He was with me and He'd never leave me. I say to myself all the time, *How people do this without the Lord by their side is beyond me.*

6

What We Didn't Know About Double Lung Transplants

I ALWAYS THOUGHT THAT once you got listed for a transplant, you'd get a call sometime soon that your organ—or two organs in my case—were ready and waiting for you. After all, the transplant team knows your life depends on it. So people often assume that you will be transplanted quickly and sent home perfectly whole again. At least, that's what we thought. Boy, did we have a lot to learn!

The demand for organs greatly outweighs the supply. Even after being accepted and listed, the waiting time can be a long one—from a few weeks to many years sometimes. Sadly, it's too long for many people. An estimated 22 people die every day in the U.S. while just waiting for a life-saving organ that never came. Too many of us want to take our organs to the grave after we die rather than leave them for someone whose life could be saved. I've yet to be able to tell the difference in an organ donor's appearance at their funeral, but I've seen the difference it can make when someone leaves their organs to someone else, especially a child. It is awesome!

Just one organ donor can save up to eight people from an early death and improve the lives of many, many more. People like you and me—with families, children, friends, and loved ones—need our organs to live longer lives. It's so easy to get registered at donatelife.net to be an organ donor. The beauty of organ donation is that most donors and recipients don't know each other. Often, they never will. I still don't know who my selfless donor was, but he and his family are heroes to me, and they always will be.

All I learned was that my donor was a 22-year-old Puerto Rican man who was in excellent shape. He was killed in a watercraft accident of some kind, like a Sea-Doo or a Jet Ski in Florida. I wrote to his family three times through LifeLink after giving them a year to mourn the loss of their loved one, but I've yet to hear back from them. I respect that. It is believed that when he died, the rest of his family moved back to Puerto Rico and didn't leave a forwarding address. So it is highly unlikely that I'll ever know anything more about my donor or them unless God sees fit. I would love to meet them, though, and thank them for his sacrifice as well as theirs.

For those who don't believe in organ donation or organ transplants, I came up with a saying: "I know that God is in favor of organ donation and organ transplants, or he wouldn't have given us interchangeable parts."

Our fight had intensified again beyond anything we could've imagined. But in our hearts, God gave us the peace that everything would be okay. It's hard to describe that, but it was something both Amy and I felt strongly about. We thanked Him for it daily. God is good!

After praying and researching day and night, I decided I didn't agree with the neuromuscular findings at Duke. I thought they were more concerned with their shiny success ratings and money than with the patient's well-being. There's also a practice referred to as cherry-picking. That's when a hospital won't take a patient who has the slightest hint of not doing well. This facility might have one of the top ratings of successful transplants in the country, on paper that is. Of course, a high rank is not too hard to achieve when you only accept surefire successful patients.

In my experience, if you pose any sort of problems or complications, no matter how small, you can be rejected for a transplant and sent away. That's what happened to me—rather unfeelingly and unprofessionally, too, I thought, since the hospital delivered the news through a form letter sent to my mailbox. Unfortunately, many medical personnel have become hardened to this rejection process. For some, a rejection letter is just another day at the office. In my case, they even added that I should quit trying, go home, and call hospice. They said I was wasting my last days on earth. I should spend this precious time with family and friends. They added that if I did go through with the transplant and survived it, I could come out of the operating room in worse shape than before I went in.

Obviously, they were wrong. In my mind, my only option was to disprove the hospital's findings that I had neuromuscular issues. That way, I hoped I could get listed by checking myself into Duke's own neurology department. There, I could be retested for the same thing that had gotten me kicked out of the hospital in the first place. The fact that their own neurological department would find me totally capable of a transplant could only add strength to my argument.

I feared I'd been cherry picked, but I couldn't be sure. That's when a hospital turns you down for no good reason other than a slight chance that you won't do well on their program, thus tarnishing their golden record of excellence. And if you don't think it exists, think again.

7

Running Out of Breath—and Time

RETESTING WHAT DUKE CALLED a neuromuscular condition required being stuck with a needle from the soles of my feet to the top of my head and back down again on both sides of my body. If that wasn't painful enough, an electric shock ran through the needle to check my nerve connection signals and reception capabilities. And yes, it hurt! The alternative was unthinkable, so I endured the pain. Amy and my daughter Rhyan watched as the medical practitioners tortured me that day. Rhyan began to cry.

After the grueling three-hour test, I point-blank asked the examiner if he had found any neuromuscular problems that would prevent me from having a double lung transplant.

"None," he said.

We were elated! I was in for sure now! It was just a matter of turning in the report to the transplant department and waiting for the call. All I had to do was continue to do well on the six-minute walks and other evaluations. We just knew I was a candidate for a transplant now. We were wrong.

After returning home, I continued my daily rehab routine, trying to stay active and build up my strength for the anticipated surgery. I would need all the physical and mental health possible to survive the surgery itself, not to mention the long post-surgical recovery process. It's hard enough to push yourself to exercise when a transplant seems likely. It's even harder to do so when you know what you're pushing so hard for will probably never happen. It was a mental challenge more than a physical one.

I discovered, not surprisingly, that both walking and breathing grew much harder. I had to increase my oxygen tank output from around two liters to about four at rest. Sometimes I had to crank it up as high as 15 liters or more upon exertion.

I was still barely able to drive myself to the hospital for pre-transplant physical therapy every morning, which was good since I had no one to drive me. A step stool got me into my truck, and an attendant got me out. I took a wheelchair into the hospital. Still, I pushed myself to go every day. My life depended on every single step I took on that treadmill, no matter how slow I walked. The more I fought to breathe on my own, the more oxygen my body required.

It would have been very easy to get discouraged and quit trying altogether. Several times, I would drive out of the rehab parking lot and directly into the emergency room parking lot located just on the other side of the hospital, only to call for someone in the emergency room to come out and get me from my truck because it was so hard to breathe that I feared my little E-cylinder oxygen tank wouldn't be enough to get me home safely before it ran out of oxygen somewhere down the highway. It's hard to call 911 when you're unconscious.

The ER team would put me on the BiPAP machine and monitor me. The BiPAP machine eliminated some of the struggles, making it much easier to inhale and exhale. After I sat there for about 30 minutes, they'd remove the BiPAP, roll me back to my truck, and send me on my way. I felt better, plus I'd saved enough oxygen in my own tank to make the 15-minute trip back home. I tried bringing an extra tank, but I found it was nearly impossible to change the tank when I was out of breath like that. Besides, it would frustrate me into a panic, and I'd never get it changed in time. I had to constantly play fast forward in my mind so I wouldn't mess up and find out much too late.

I was largely on my own now, facing a monster I'd never known before. I couldn't call Amy every time I had a problem. She worked 25 miles away, and it was important for her to work all she could. If I did get accepted for a transplant, Amy would have to leave her job to be my caregiver for at least six months after my surgery. Besides, our insurance depended on her job, and we needed that health insurance desperately now.

Have you ever priced a double lung transplant? It costs between $155,000 and $785,000. That price doesn't include pre-testing or post-op and follow-up care once home. Plus, we would have to cover living expenses and all that goes with it in an apartment for six months. Coming home wasn't an option. I had to sign a contract that said I would remain near the hospital where I'd gotten my transplant for six months following the surgery. No questions asked. So the money adds up, or goes down, I should say. Oh … and a set of lungs doesn't come with a money-back guarantee if they fail. You take what you can get and you're happy for them.

I called Duke soon after the neuromuscular test to tell them what I considered good news—their very own department said they were wrong the first time they evaluated me. The transplant team agreed to see me again. Amy and I felt optimistic and confident. We couldn't wait to get the test behind us and get on with the program. We did not get the reception we expected from Duke. It wasn't long before I received another rejection letter, but it was for a different reason this time. They just kept coming up with reasons to reject me as quickly as I could disprove their last reason. It felt like hell had determined to deny me this transplant no matter what. Still, Amy and I believed strongly that God had already given us the confirmation that a transplant would come for us. With God moving in our lives, we couldn't quit. We wouldn't quit!

Healthier Times for Me

Kokopelli Sun
Cherry Grove, SC
Paddleboarding 2017

Norris Sign Works shop sign
I made out of an old sawmill blade.
Sadly we would end up closing the shop
for good after I got IPF.

Norris Sign Works, before
IPF closed the doors.

For years I'd enjoyed the art of freehand lettering
but the anti-rejection meds caused my hands to
tremble, so I was never able to do it again.

My hand's too shakey now.
I DESIGNED & BUILT THIS GATE MYSELF BY HAND -BUDDY NORRIS

I created this from some old stained-glass windows I retrieved from a dumpster plus a statue of Jesus. Then I added lights. After IPF I would never have the strength to do a project of this magnitude again. But I am thankful still just to be here to observe it. God is Good!

THE 10-HOUR LUNG TRANSPLANT SURGERY DAMAGED MY VOCAL CORDS TO THE POINT THAT I COULD NO LONGER SING. IT WAS HARD TO ACCEPT.

I taught 8th grade at my church

LOCK IN 2000
YOUTH A
SUNDAY SCHOOL CLASS

Last time I sang in the studio wearing oxygen. That's when I Knew that singing was over too. This was pre-transplant.

Amy and I used to love biking until I became too sick to ride anymore

Fishing was a love of mine until I had to be so careful of germs and bacteria

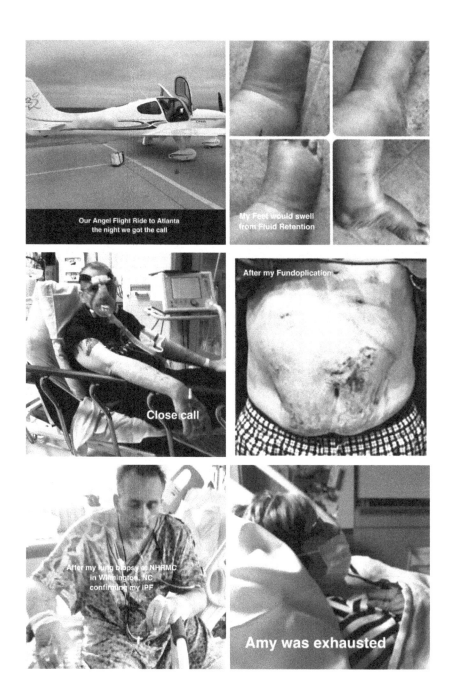

Our Angel Flight Ride to Atlanta the night we got the call

My Feet would swell from Fluid Retention

Close call

After my Fundoplication

After my lung biopsy at NHRMC in Wilmington, NC confirming my IPF

Amy was exhausted

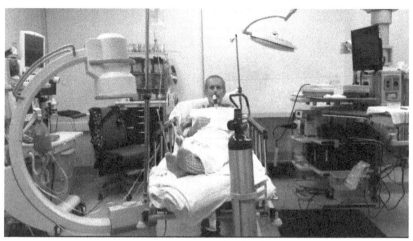

BRONCOSCOPY

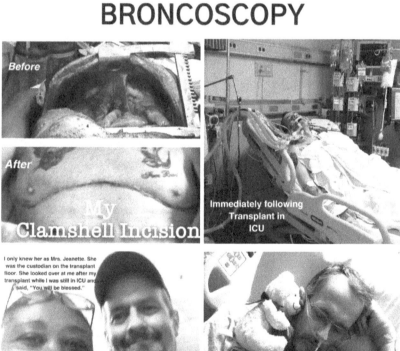

Before

After

My Clamshell Incision

Immediately following Transplant in ICU

I only knew her as Mrs. Jeanette. She was the custodian on the transplant floor. She looked over at me after my transplant while I was still in ICU and said, "You will be blessed."

A gift from Home

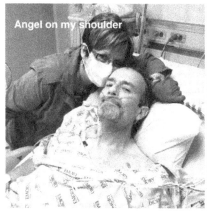

Angel on my shoulder

...and I remember thinking, this is Love
-Rhyan Norris

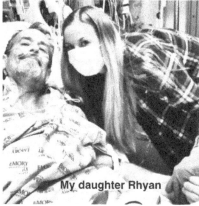

My daughter Rhyan

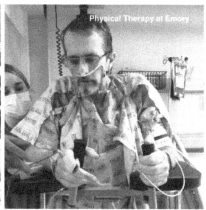

Physical Therapy at Emory

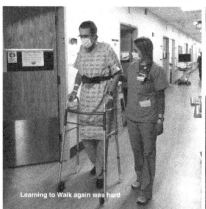

Learning to Walk again was hard

Stephanie was my awesome PT at Emory

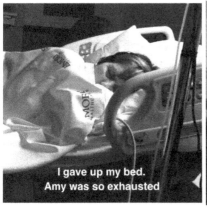

I gave up my bed.
Amy was so exhausted

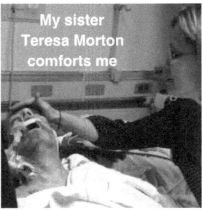

My sister
Teresa Morton
comforts me

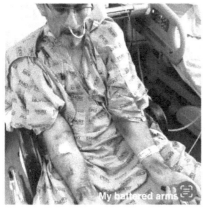

My battered arms

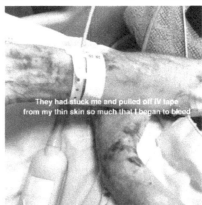

They had stuck me and pulled off IV tape
from my thin skin so much that I began to bleed

Mama (Barbara Norris) &
my sister (Melissa Etheridge)

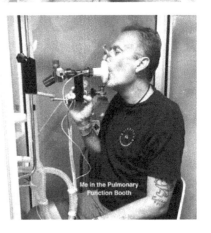

Me in the Pulmonary
Function Booth

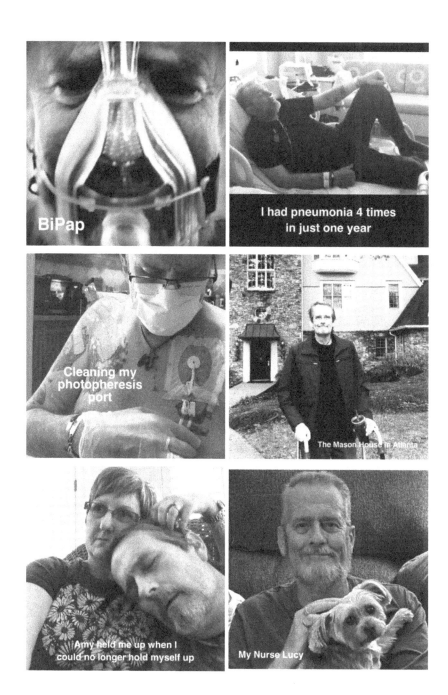

BiPap

I had pneumonia 4 times in just one year

Cleaning my photopheresis port

The Mason House in Atlanta

Amy held me up when I could no longer hold myself up

My Nurse Lucy

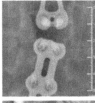

3x Back Surgeries &
2x Neck Surgeries have
left me in constant pain and
much stiffness

BONE DENSITY HAS BEEN
GREATLY REDUCED DUE TO THE
TAKING OF SO MANY STEROIDS POST
TRANSPLANT

PIC·COLLAGE

My cousin
Frankie Norris
visited us and prayed regularly
for my healing.
His prayers were answered.
Thanks Frankie!

First time climbing to the Top!

First Outing in Atlanta. The Varsity

Daddy

We couldn't have done this without the Support and Prayers of Good Friends

Good Friends & Family at The Mason House Atlanta

Family Support

Tammy Berry
Thank you for all of your help getting us closer to my transplant

My cousin, STEVE NORRIS Prayed for me and was anointed with oil for me every Sunday at Andrew's Chapel Methodist Church in Hickman's Crossroads NC

My good friend Chase has been an inspiration of strength to me for some time

friends Beth and
CHARLES BINGENHEIMER.
Charles "BING" payed the
ultimate price for contracting IPF.
We must find a cure.

My Sister & her husband.
Teresa & the late Todd Morton.
My sister is a living organ donor. She
gave Todd one of her Kidneys.
Unfortunately we lost Todd anyway.

MR. MARVIN BENNETT
was such a huge influence
in my life as a Christian.
We miss you Pop.

Rev. Phil Norris
& Andrew's Chapel
Meth. Church
prayed for me
weekly

Pastor Bob Weathers of FBCS
was our pastor during my
illness. He was amazing!

The youth at our church First Baptist
Church of Shallotte came to visit when
I could no longer attend church. Thanks
Michael Borton

When I could no longer attend Church at First Baptist Church of Shallotte, First Baptist came to me in our yard.

In 2014 I survived a DOUBLE LUNG TRANSPLANT

Please be an Organ Donor at donatelife.net

That's why God gave us interchangeable parts!

Signs I made for fellow transplant warriors

Vicki Artz, also a recipient of a double lung transplant, and I had A donate life exhibit at FBCS

Me at 7 years post transplant riding a bike about 12 miles a day until I went into Chronic Rejection

My Girls 2021

Me and my Family believe laughter can cure anything! Sisters Melissa Etheridge & Teresa Morton along with my Mama In Atlanta

My Angel

Everybody loves our sweet Amy!

I held my granddaughter for the first time because of an Organ Donor

I wouldn't know my great nephew Noah if not for my selfless organ donor

Eisley and her Papa
3 years post transplant

#NeverGiveUp

A constant reminder I wear everyday

BE STRONGER THAN THE STORM

My first time back on Ocean Isle Beach, NC after my transplant 6 months earlier

Breathe

MADE WITH FONT CANDY

Second Wind

I designed this Logo after I'd had my transplant and had it tattooed on my arm.

My Tattoo

11·25·14

Dr. Barton Schneyer,
My top-notch pulmonologist
In Southport, NC

"perseverance was the
key to Success"

Dr. Leonard Lobo
My awesome pulmonologist
at UNC Chapel Hill, NC

Dr. David Neujahr
My Amazing Pulmonologist
who was instrumental in getting me
accepted for a transplant at Emory,
Atlanta, Ga.

Hillary & Adam Thompson

Hillary and Adam have been
and still are my family physicians.
They were with me before and since my
transplant. They've always had
my back.

Rena Scates,
MSN, RN, FNP

For
making the hurt
not hurt so much.
Thanks!

Christina White,
Our lung transplant
Coordinator at UNC
Hospital in Chapel Hill,
NC
"Tina, you Rock!"

DR. SETH FORCE performed my double lung transplant on Nov. 25, 2014 at Emory in Atlanta

8

A Short Guide to Taking a Shower with IPF

EVEN MY SHOWERS IN THE morning required a lot of preplanning.

Just sitting up took my breath away. After I sat up in the mornings, I would sit on the side of the bed and just wait for my breathing to get easier. It usually took 30 minutes or more of heaving for air while leaning back against the headboard until my breathing finally subsided to the best it was going to ever get (which wasn't great by any means).

Once I adjusted to sitting and my breath returned, I'd slip off my pants and shirt. Doing those two things took a lot of oxygen, oxygen I couldn't easily inhale because my lungs were beginning to harden from the scar tissue inside. Bending over to pull my pants off the end of my feet was the worst. Just bending at all made it harder to breathe.

Eventually, I'd stand up. You wouldn't think it takes much oxygen to stand up, but it does. That sudden rush of blood to my legs took a lot of oxygen, and I could feel it getting harder to breathe again until my body had time to adjust to this new position. Then it would get a little easier if I could withstand the wait before having to sit back down. I've learned that it takes oxygen to do anything. Even the simple things I'd done before, like brushing my teeth, required a lot of oxygen, so I would have to do it in stages.

I couldn't waste much time just standing there. I did all of this while pulling an oxygen tank.

Once I was up, I immediately had to start the 15 short, calculated steps from my bed to the shower. I couldn't walk too fast because walking fast required extra oxygen.

Once I got to the bathroom, I had to sit on the stool we'd placed by the shower stall and catch my breath. Then I'd step over the short wall of the tub, which seemed like it was a mile high, and sit again on a different stool we'd placed inside the shower stall itself. Finally, I would reach up and turn the water on, then immediately drop both arms back in my lap to conserve oxygen. Because even that, as small as it may seem, would make my breathing harder again, and that would cost me more time just sitting and waiting to catch my breath. Yes, I know! It was crazy!

The actual washing began slowly. If I gradually slid the loofah up and down my arms and legs, then I could go longer before becoming winded. But if I sped it up, even the least little bit, I would run out of breath quickly. It could take me up to two hours to finish washing, most of it just rest time.

I wasn't done then either. I had to take the big step up and out of the shower stall. I always dreaded picking my heavy leg up and over onto the floor mat waiting below. It was hard enough standing on two feet, much less supporting my weight on one foot for the one second it took to step out of the shower. Every day, I feared I'd fall, but praise God, it never happened.

After my shower came drying-off time. I had to hold the weight of a towel in my hands while moving it around my body slowly. Sounds funny? Maybe so, but in my condition, that towel felt like it weighed 100 pounds, so drying off tired me out rapidly; even when I was sitting down, I had to do it in stages.

Finally, I'd begin the long 15-step walk back to my waiting recliner, where I'd rest and get dressed. In the early days of IPF, I forgot to check my oxygen tank level once before starting my shower, and I ran out of oxygen while still in the bathroom. Nobody could hear me call them because I could barely speak anymore. I had no choice but to hurry back to my recliner, which I knew would only make me struggle more for air, and then also remove the empty cylinder and replace it with a full tank. I was in a panic, worried that I'd pass out from lack of oxygen before I completed the tank switch and Amy would find me there.

For the most part, though, I tried to remain cool-headed, telling myself to calm down and make every move count. All along, my lungs screamed for air. I told myself that was the last time that would ever happen, but of course, I did it a few more times.

Once I even ran out of oxygen while having an MRI. And you know how long it takes them to get you out of that machine. Plus, when they slowly did get me out, I knew I still had to switch tanks to breathe again. I thought I had plenty of oxygen to complete the MRI, but I forgot how much more oxygen it took for me to breathe lying down. I ran out just short of finishing. Then to make matters worse, I had to repeat the test because it was imperative that they have the results if we were to move forward. I never let that happen again; the next time, I was ready. Lack of air makes a lasting impression on you.

I'm proud to say that I gave myself my own showers and dressed myself right up until my transplant. I even considered it all a part of my daily workout, but eventually, showering became nearly impossible. I'm very modest, but I would have been forced to ask Amy for help with showers if I had declined any more.

After I showered, I spent most of the day in my chair, either just on oxygen or maybe even on my BiPAP machine, while researching or making phone calls to other transplant hospitals. When I felt my strongest, I'd take on the challenge of getting to my treadmill on the other side of the room. I might even tackle the challenge of not only getting to the treadmill but also getting on it. That's right. Sometimes I was too tired once I made it to the treadmill to even get on it, much less walk. But every physical activity could be considered part of my daily exercise, so nothing was wasted time. It didn't matter if I only walked for three minutes or ten minutes, as long as I walked and at the same time saved enough strength to get back to my chair alone. It was all better than doing nothing at all like my body wanted me to do so badly.

9

It Was a Miracle from God!

November 24, 2014

SOMETIMES MIRACLES COME disguised as disasters. We don't quite understand them until later. Only God could have orchestrated the things that fell into place this particular day.

I had been hospitalized with pneumonia for two days while the doctors gave me antibiotics and breathing treatments. The hospital released me around noon on Monday, November 24, 2014. Amy was at work, but as soon as the doctor discharged me, I let her know. She arrived at the hospital within 45 minutes.

Amy got me home, and I had only made it to the bedroom. I was sitting on the bed with our dog Lucy when within the hour, the phone rang. We both looked at the phone's caller ID and recognized the number as an Atlanta area code. It was the transplant team at Emory. My lungs were ready. We looked at the clock. It was 2:33 p.m. Had the team called just hours earlier, I would have been in the hospital here at home still. But now I was feeling a lot better because they had pumped me full of antibiotics, which would now serve another purpose—to get me stronger and protect me during what was about to happen. God had a plan. Hallelujah!!

Amy packed only the bare necessities in a small bag. We headed to Myrtle Beach to the small airport where Angel Flight, a volunteer medical flight service, met us around 5:30 p.m. to fly us to DeKalb Peachtree Airport in Atlanta. It now seemed so surreal, like a dream I was watching unfold in front of me

Angel Flight staff members were amazing. They helped us send our departure and arrival times to the transplant team in Atlanta. The volunteer pilot who flew his small, personal, single-engine plane from Durham to Myrtle Beach and then to Atlanta went above and beyond the call of duty just to help me get in and out of the plane (as described in chapter one) with oxygen tanks in tow. I found out after the transplant that I was the pilot and plane owner's first flight since signing on with Angel Flight. After the bumpy flight, Amy and I arrived in Atlanta at about 7:45 p.m. We took a waiting taxi to Emory Hospital. Once he heard why we were in Atlanta, the taxi cab driver refused any money for his services.

Our transplant coordinator had given us instructions to go to the ER and inform them we were there for a bilateral lung transplant. They would fast-track me through the ER. However, getting through the ER wasn't as smooth as we'd hoped. I did get fast-tracked through admission though. They took us by elevator to the third floor, where I was to be prepped for surgery. Amy was taken to a waiting area where she was given information regarding how the next hours would unfold.

Within 30 minutes of them getting me prepped, Amy got to come back and see me. The transplant surgeon was still on the way to the hospital, so we had more time than expected. Soon, though, the nurse who was talking with us looked up and said, "Here comes the surgeon now."

Amy got to meet the surgeon before they took me back. I told Amy I loved her, and she whispered it back to me. Then we said our goodbyes, not knowing if we'd ever see each other again or not. The team had me prepped and in the OR by 11:00 p.m.

A whirlwind of emotions—fear, happiness, and anticipation—I overtook me. It was all out of my hands now. All my efforts to save my life had come down to this moment. God and other people would have to take it from here. I was just along for the ride now. Right then, I felt the presence of God with me in a supernatural way that I can't explain even to this day. It was very comforting, and it gave me a welcome peace and serenity.

10

My First Deep Breath in Three Years

AMY SAT ALONE IN THE huge waiting room. My family, driving in from North Carolina, wouldn't arrive until 1:00 a.m. I'd have felt better if they'd been with her when I went back, but that was out of their control since they had to drive the whole six hours. But Amy is tough. If anyone could handle this, it was Amy Norris. She'd been my constant strength through it all and had taught me how to be strong. Now, I might never see her again.

I later learned that she had what she calls "a moment." As she tells it, when she was first taken to the waiting area, there were only about five people already in there, people she didn't know. They soon left, however, and she was all alone in a huge waiting room. That's when it hit her. She'd always had an unwavering belief that I'd be transplanted. She'll tell you that God had given her peace about it during all the rejection letters coming in. Amy knew what it meant to praise Him in the storm, as the Casting Crowns song tells us. But sitting in a hospital waiting room six hours away from home all by herself in the middle of the night, she thought, "Okay, God, I've never wavered in believing you said Buddy would be transplanted, but you never said he would survive the transplant."

Today, Amy says that was the devil wanting her to doubt God. You don't go there with her; she just prayed some more and went back to keeping various family and friends updated on what was happening by phone. Soon my parents, Gene and Barbara Norris, and my two beautiful sisters, Teresa Morton and Melissa Etheridge, arrived. Amy brought them up to date on my surgery. My daughter, Rhyan Norris, was coming alone with our car from the Myrtle Beach airport where she'd dropped us off. We were going to need it soon—we hoped.

Ten hours after they took me back, I woke up in the ICU's recovery room. I was still heavily sedated, so it took me a couple of minutes to realize where I was and what had just taken place. Reality hit soon. I'd had a double lung transplant! Someone else's lungs were inside of me now, and most importantly, I was still alive. I didn't panic as I took inventory of my present situation. *Okay, I'm transplanted. I have a large tube down my throat. My hands are tied down, so I don't pull it out.* I was good with all of that because I was still very sedated, I guess, but still aware of everything. I'd expected it all, and I'd prepared myself mentally as much as one can for the moment when I would wake up. Now here it was. *Don't panic now,* I told myself. Just got to be calm and stay focused.

Then I heard Amy's sweet voice say, "You did it, Shug. It's over. It's all over. You can breathe now."

Apparently, I had been shallow breathing for so long that I didn't realize I'd stopped taking big, full breaths at some point. I remember hearing nurses telling Amy and my sisters to keep encouraging me to take deep breaths and expand those new lungs.

"Just take a deep breath, Buddy," Amy said.

Eyes closed, I did as she told me. For the first time in three years, I took a deep breath, and it was the most amazing feeling I've ever had! It was, without a doubt, truly a miracle! God's peace in my soul assured me that everything was going to be alright now.

My daughter Rhyan told me she was there, and I heard her say, "I love you, Daddy; you did it!" My two younger sisters, Melissa and Sissy, were by my bed, also speaking words of love and encouragement like always. They'd all been there since this journey had first begun four years earlier. Mama and Daddy came into the ICU, too, but Mama wasn't prepared for how I would look. I later learned that she started to cry and left the ICU saying, "I didn't know he'd look like that." When I saw the first picture Amy took of me right after the transplant in the ICU, I could easily understand how Mama must have felt seeing me in that condition. There were drain tubes and IVs, and I was on a vent too, I think. It was a good thing I'd had the transplant, of course, but I didn't look like a good thing, that's for sure.

After I later requested the operative notes from the surgeon during my surgery, I learned just what the surgical team had been up to for the last 10 hours. Using a clamshell incision, which is a cut from armpit to armpit across the chest, even sawing through the sternum, they'd pretty much cut me in half and forced my ribs to remain open with two big clamps. The surgeon had spent six hours working on my already-dead left lung and four hours working on my right lung, removing and replacing each of them with the donor's lungs. My right lung, I learned, had been functioning at just 17% before the surgery. With only 17% lung function, what kept me alive and moving? I'll tell you what and who. God had! Like only God could!

All our prayers had been answered.

11

He's Trying to Kill Me!

I RELAXED AND SLEPT MOST of the first day. But that night came the unexpected and terrifying hallucinations.

In the first one, a man in scrubs came into the ICU, walked up to my bedside, and started angrily shouting at me. He said something about me owing him money and that I'd been ignoring him. He was loud and he was very angry. I knew my hands were helplessly tied to the bed—totally defenseless and vulnerable to him. It felt so real that I sweated with fear. My hospital gown was soaking wet from sweat. My heart was beating so hard, it felt like it would jump out of my chest. The same man reappeared at least two more nights, each time doing the same thing. He may have been a hallucination, but to me, he was as real as everything else around me.

Since he appeared to be wearing scrubs, I decided the unknown man was an employee of the hospital, a nurse maybe. I couldn't talk because of the vent tube down my throat, so I couldn't call out for help or tell anyone what I was seeing. On the second night, my sisters popped in unexpectedly at 3:00 in the morning. They said that they couldn't sleep and had decided to come to see me. I'd never been so happy to hear their voices in my life before then. I made writing motions, so one of them handed me a pen and a notepad tablet. I carefully wrote, "Call the police. He's trying to kill me. Fortunately, as soon I began to come off the pain meds, the "man" slowly disappeared. I was happy to see him go.

I came out of surgery around 9:00 a.m. on Wednesday, November 25, 2014. They took me off the vent but left the tube in, in case I needed it again since I was breathing on my own. But that could change. For two days, I'd had no nutrition. My medical team did not want to let it go past that. They had put a feeding tube through my nose into my stomach to give me nutrition. I also had to have a bronchoscopy, which wasn't unusual. That's a test where they go through your mouth and into your lungs with a tube with a camera on the end of it. They're searching for infections, closed airways, or anything else that doesn't look right. Little did I know I'd be having a lot more of those later. The bronch, as we call it in the lung transplant world, showed no issues. So far, my new lungs were holding their own. Then came Thursday night.

I started having trouble breathing. A nurse noticed swelling over my right collar bone area and suspected fluid retention. The right lung had collapsed, and fluid had been building up there. They had to cut new incisions on the sides of my chest and reinsert four drain lines back into my lungs to allow fluid to escape correctly again and then reinflate my lung like a balloon.

My breathing improved throughout Saturday. The team was weaning me off pain meds, and I grew more alert as the day went on. At no time was I ever in even the slightest pain. I didn't expect that at all, but it's true. By Sunday, I was aware of everything but would doze off if left alone.

Monday was an important day. Two drain tubes, out of the four total, had to come out. Around 7:30 a.m., medical staff members were already checking my blood gasses. At 9:00 a.m., it was time for the breathing tube down my throat itself to come out. And with one firm pull, it was out! This was monumental because, within an hour, I was finally able to talk a little bit, although I was hoarse. The good news was that I was still breathing on my own and with my new lungs. Of course, my good news was someone else's tragedy. It was hard not to think of the donor and his family during Thanksgiving and Christmas. As difficult as it was for our family to be away from home for so long, at least we were all still together. The donor's family was broken apart by death. We prayed for them throughout the season.

The physical rehab tech had me on my feet the day after the transplant. With a tall walker, I was able to walk across the ICU floor to the other side of the room and back much easier than I'd expected.

Seven days after my transplant, I moved into a private room where I started to feel much weaker than I did in the ICU for some reason. I couldn't even stand under my own power, much less walk across the room.

But the therapist had plans to change that and first get me walking again as quickly as possible. She was persistent about it too. I worked with her every single day. Before long, I dreaded hearing her footsteps coming down the long hallway. I knew I had to work with her, though, if I were to ever get stronger and walk again. So I pushed myself hard to achieve my goals in every therapy session. Her name was Stephanie, and she was awesome.

At first, she only had me stand up and sit back down. Doesn't sound like much? Oh, it was though! Soon she'd have me stand up and take one step and sit back down. Eventually, I was walking down the hallway with the help of a walker. Then, I did it without the walker. You get the picture. It was a long, brutal, and unforgiving road back.

Food became another issue. After surgery, I was on a feeding tube. For 16 days straight, I ate nothing solid. I can't tell how much I looked forward to eating real food again. First, though, I had to pass the dreaded swallow test.

Since everything in my throat had been detached and reattached when I had the transplant, swallowing had to be tested. They always say, and it's quite gross, that the first phlegm you cough up isn't yours. If something went wrong in the process of swallowing, I could aspirate food or liquid into my lungs or choke, which could be deadly for me. The tester gave me barium stirred up with peaches to eat. They called it peaches and cream, but don't let the name fool you. It was a far cry from tasting like any peaches and cream I'd ever eaten. It was more like peaches and crap. It wasn't even close to having a pleasant taste at all. When I would swallow, you could watch the mixture going down my throat into my stomach on a sort-of x-ray machine that was placed beside me. I hoped everything looked good because I was ready for some good food.

Somewhere around my fourth or fifth attempt, it finally happened. I swallowed the barium and watched as it slowly made its way down my throat and into my stomach normally again. Success! Now I could finally eat real food. The first thing they brought me was a fruit plate full of fresh-cut fruit—watermelon, cantaloupe, apples, and kiwis. Normally I'm not a fan of kiwi, but that day I was. I didn't stop eating until the plate was empty, and then I begged for more, which they generously provided.

I can't say enough good things about the nurses on the pulmonary floor at Emory. They took fantastic care of me during my 23-day stay in the hospital. Those nurses went above and beyond duty and became like family. So did all the doctors on my transplant team there. They became like family to us, too. We had been rejected by Duke hospital three times, Cleveland Clinic once, and Pittsburg Hospital once. Now, we knew it was all for a reason. God wanted us to be at Emory University Hospital in Atlanta, Georgia, and praise God, that's exactly where we were.

God used the team at Emory to save my life even after all the other hospitals had given up on me and told me that I'd never even survive the surgery, and if I did survive it, I would be in a much worse condition when I came out than before I went in. Some of them even bluntly recommended that we call in hospice because it wouldn't be much longer for me on this earth now and that I shouldn't waste any more time running around trying to get accepted and listed for a double lung transplant. But God had other plans for me, plans that would prove once again that nothing is impossible with God. Nothing. I'm reminded of a quote I heard once: "The difficult we do immediately. The impossible just takes a little longer."

12

The Transplant Trade-Off

AFTER SURGERY, WE STILL had a way to go, at least one week in ICU and then two more weeks in a private room.

When I was discharged, we stayed at The Mason House, Emory's housing center available to organ recipients and family members upon discharge. It's kind of a space in between hospital life and real life—a middle-of-the-road transition place to live temporarily, if you will. We stayed there for about five weeks. Being with other lung, liver, kidney, or heart transplant recipients and their families and/or caregivers. It proved to be a very rewarding experience.

Eventually, we moved to an apartment for the remaining months in Atlanta. Altogether, we stayed in Atlanta for six months. This was mandatory. When we were accepted for transplant, we were required to sign a contract agreeing to a six-month stay inside the city limits and close to Emory in case of an emergency. Amy was with me the whole time. God had blessed me with the most wonderful wife and caregiver a man could ever ask for.

Most people don't understand how a transplant works. They think that once a person receives a transplant—lung, heart, kidney, or other organs—you are magically healed and will be back to being the same person you were before you were diagnosed with the disease that required an organ transplant. Not the case! You have a quality of life return, but you trade your day-to-day life for all kinds of anti-rejection medications for the rest of your natural life. Various supplements to replace the naturally occurring ones in the body are also now required daily. Depending on how your body adapts to these changes, you could end up taking medications to control diabetes, high blood pressure, and well … the list goes on.

I was on 30+ pills a day for the first few months. Depending on lab reports, these pills would be adjusted to ensure that my body was not rejecting the lungs. Yes, my body knows that these lungs are not the ones I was born with. They are intruders, and my body will constantly try to reject them if I live. I must have blood drawn monthly for the rest of my life like clockwork to monitor all kinds of levels to keep these airbags functioning at their best. Other organs have taken a toll as a result of these medications, especially my kidneys, and I have seen the effects get bigger as I get further out from the transplant. Most transplant recipients can find themselves on dialysis and in need of new kidneys at some point since it's so hard for the kidneys to continually process these anti-rejection meds, like Tacrolimus, for example. My kidneys have taken an expectedly hard hit. I pretty much came out of surgery in stage three chronic kidney disease. My kidneys are always monitored monthly by watching my creatinine levels. Mine has been running too high for eight years, which is not good. The thought of dialysis in my future followed by a kidney transplant isn't a nice thought, but it's one that could easily become a reality at some point. You just learn not to dwell on thoughts like these and trust that God didn't heal you just to leave you hanging now and that He's still in control. Nothing happens until He says so.

After my transplant, life is very different on a day-to-day basis in a lot of ways. Since the anti-rejection meds knock down my immune system, I am left vulnerable to everything from a simple cold to the flu, but one of the most alarming is cancer. In other words, the cells in my body that are designed to protect me before I can get any sicker—and get me well when I do get sick—don't work properly anymore. Diseases like cancer, once they start in my body, get a good foothold and are more likely to do more damage, unlike someone whose immune system is not compromised.

Since I went into chronic rejection a few years back, I had to have a Campath infusion, which knocked my immune system down even lower than it already was. It did, however, slow the rejection down enough that I'm still here. For now. For that, I'm most thankful and blessed. It seems like for every good remedy, there was a bad price to pay. So you pick the lesser of the two evils and just go with that.

I've already had skin cancer more than once, though, and I must wear a face mask most of the time, along with sunblock and a hat and long sleeve shirt. It's kind of funny that Amy and I were wearing a face mask in public even before COVID-19 came into the picture. Now everybody wears one. I also try to stay out of crowds as much as possible. I will roll the dice occasionally and go out and do things just like everybody else does, but it's rare. Although I did go through this to live, not to just sit at home in a bubble. I've learned that you must use common sense.

13

God's Not Done Yet

GOD HAS BEEN GOOD TO ME. I'm not only referring to my double lung transplant either. You see, that's not the first time God has spared my life. When I was only six years old, I stepped in front of a moving car coming down a paved highway near my grandparents' tobacco farm in Ash, NC. The impact sent me flying. I skidded across a dirt driveway on my back. That's a pretty good lick for a little boy to survive, but it happened. All I recall about that day is chasing my cousin Steve Norris across the highway without looking first. I turned to my left and saw the hood of a red car which now was about chin high to me and only inches away. Then the lights went out. That's about all I remember.

Steve still recalls that I went airborne. My sweet grandmama Oleta, who was walking with us and some of my other cousins, dropped to her knees and could only point in my direction. She could barely utter the word "dead" over and over. My grandaddy Leon, who was there by now, picked me up in his arms and carried me back to his house, which was only about two city blocks away. My aunt Lona met us at the house, and then they loaded me up in their car.

I was awake now, and I remember being in the backseat with my head in Aunt Lona's lap. They rushed me to the closest hospital, which was about 35 miles away in Wilmington, NC. To make a long story short, my mama and daddy drove from Riegelwood, NC, where we lived then, and met us at the hospital's ER where I was being examined. The nurse put pure old Merthiolate on the scrapes on my back I'd received from the gravel on the road. It was almost pure alcohol, which made me scream. That made Daddy very angry. He told the nurse never to do that again!

I was released only a couple of hours later. I don't remember even having x-rays, but I could have just forgotten. Only God could perform a miracle like that! Sometime later, I was told that another woman, who was also walking along that same road where I was struck that day, also dropped to her knees almost unnoticed. She lifted her hands toward the sky and began to pray to Jesus loudly. I'm satisfied that's why I'm still here today too.

I won't even tell the whole story about the close drowning experience I had while out surfing at Ocean Isle Beach, NC one cold winter day with a faulty wetsuit. Suffice it to say that God heard my cries that day too, and He literally lifted me up out of the angry waves and set my feet on dry land. Praise his name!

So yes, I do find myself asking God, "Why me? Why have you spared my life so many times, Lord? Call it survivor's guilt, maybe. I'm not sure. But why am I still here after coming close to death all these times in my 60 years on this earth?" I even walked away from five, count them FIVE, car wrecks where the vehicles were all totaled, and I didn't even have a scratch. None of the accidents were my fault. I guess it's like people say, "God's not finished with me yet."

I even fell 25 feet from the top of a tree on a zip line to the hard ground below that knocked me unconscious. When I woke up, I had tunnel vision for a day with an excruciating headache.

A dear friend of mine, Mr. Marvin Bennett, once told me that no matter what life gives you or what the doctors say, you WILL NOT, CANNOT leave this world until God says so—plain and simple. And all of man's statistics about death can't change that. God loves each of us the same, no matter who we are. He has different purposes for each of us in His big plan while we're here.

14

My Tribute

THERE'S ONE MAJOR REQUIREMENT for anyone to receive a double lung transplant—you must have a caregiver. It's not optional. It's mandatory. And with good reason. I understand that now more than ever. I was blessed with the best caregiver God could ever give anybody—and she's my wife, Amy Norris. She has been and, twenty-seven years later, still is the best of everything in my life, even 12 years after I was first diagnosed with IPF in 2010. Next to God, she's the reason I'm still alive today. There's no question about it.

After I became so helpless early in the game, Amy took over the work of my legs, my arms, my lungs, and really every part of me. It was an indescribably huge job that I didn't see coming at first. Before long, though, I became almost totally dependent on her help to get anything done at all. She's driven me literally thousands of miles to doctor's appointments, evaluations, MRIs, CT scans, lung x-rays, PFTs, and monthly blood labs. Amy has taken me to clinic visits every month, most of them more than a six-hour drive away from our home in just one direction, which also required loading enough O2 bottles in the back for the entire trip there and back. She's had them fall and break her toe, and she's even had to get stitches in her forehead from falling onto the concrete driveway at our house while retrieving an oxygen bottle from the car when I needed one ASAP. She got it to me too, blood and all and dripping wet, before tending to herself. The list goes on and on. To me, she is the true warrior in this story, not me, and I love her dearly.

Driving me was the easiest part for her, if there was an easy part. After we got to wherever we had driven, Amy's labor of love had just begun because I could only sit and watch, unable to help her in the least. Now, Amy had to push me in a wheelchair—sometimes for miles a day through different hospitals and anywhere else I had to be to make this whole transplant thing come together. Because of setbacks, even after the transplant, she's had to continue to do these things for me now.

To this day, Amy has never complained. Not even once. She's done it all with a smile while hiding her tears from me, having only my best interest in mind. Anyone who knows Amy knows that she never thinks about herself or neglects me or what I need for even one second. I have to make her take care of herself, and I've made a promise to do my best to take care of her as much as I humanly can.

At eight years post-transplant, as of 2022, I'm not much help to her anymore as I was before I became sick. But I try to do as much as I can without always calling on her. Sometimes it's hard not to feel like a burden to her. Amy always reassures me that I'm not a burden at all and that she knows I'd do the same for her if our roles were reversed. And I would. But I don't want her to ever go through anything like this to find out though. We have a wonderful life together, and all our experiences, both good and bad, have only brought us closer together and closer to God. It has not pushed us apart, although we've had our heated moments just like everybody else in a high-stress situation. But we always had one common denominator—I know how much she loves me too. She shows me every day. I am proud to say that 2022 will make 27 years of marriage for us against all odds. And I do mean ALL odds. God has been so good to us.

I sit here today, weak and short of breath. My back and hip are constantly hurting from unending and unforgiving pain due to osteoporosis as well as existing back injuries. Some from medicine-induced problems and some from the years of construction work along with the years of working in my business, Norris Sign Works, building my own billboards and lifting plywood. I can't help but close my eyes, go back in time, and remember how hard the last two years really have been after having six good years post-transplant.

But if you're considering having a transplant and wondering, yes, I'd do it all again in a minute. I got to see my beautiful daughter, Rhyan Elisabeth, get married, and I got to meet my first grandchild—a beautiful, loving granddaughter, Eisley Jane Paradee—for the first time, who we love very much. There have been many other happy moments as well, like my and Amy's 25th silver wedding anniversary.

Amy and I both have had numerous opportunities to help others—without forcing our opinions on anybody unless we're asked—who might be facing the same battles we did. We try to offer a little bit of what God can do for them along with some encouragement and advice in hopes it might make their journey a little easier than ours was. That's the purposes of this book. It's been a learning experience from the beginning. One of trial and error, I guess you could say.

My life before the transplant—a carefree life of coming and going as I pleased before I was diagnosed with idiopathic pulmonary fibrosis is somewhat just a memory now. Although it's still a happy life, it's true that it will never be what it once was before IPF, but praise God I'm still here today and kicking. One thing I lost was the ability to sing at all. Before my transplant, I sang solos in churches often. It was a love of mine, and I can't tell you that it was easy to accept losing it. I kept thinking God would give me back my singing ability eventually after my vocal cords healed from so many bronchs, along with a tube in my throat through my vocal cords for the 10 hours straight of surgery that glorious day. But it never came back. It wasn't easy to accept then, and it still isn't. I don't think I'll ever get over that one loss, no matter how trivial it may sound. But in my heart, I know there was a reason, and I thank God for all the years He allowed me to use His precious gift to me for His Glory.

I know my old life existed. I remember the good times. I remember being a big, strong man. I always prided myself on being health conscious. I was able to do pretty much whatever I wanted to do physically and was proud of my accomplishments back then. But one day, while I was still in the Emory Hospital, I made many attempts to get up on my own and walk to my bathroom, finally managing to get there. I caught the first glimpse of myself in a long time in the mirror from the side. Oh my, I was so, so thin! I looked like a prisoner from a concentration camp. It turns out I was almost 100 pounds lighter than before I first became ill. My hospital gown hung straight down. From the side view, I appeared to have no human form at all, like a skeleton.

Seven years later, I'm pushing around a walker and sitting down and resting a lot. Some days I get by with just a cane. But I find myself very short of breath daily now if I exert myself, due to a recent paralyzed diaphragm on the right side, which was a result of my phrenic nerve being damaged during my third back surgery. My back pain has gotten worse from all the steroid medicines eating away at my bone density, and the pain is especially severe in my hip. I now have osteoporosis there.

Keep in mind that the first year post-transplant was pretty good. I was breathing and walking fine for the most part. I even bought a bicycle and started riding daily, sometimes for miles at a time even. I was kicking butt! But the last couple of years have been filled with unforeseen problems. Most of them, doctors told me early on, would probably come one day. They were right. I have to take so many steroids and anti-rejection meds that simply walking has almost become a thing of the past, and I don't think that I'll ever again walk like I used to. When I stand or even slightly move, the bones in my back and neck crack and pop like they're coming apart. I still try though.

In May 2022, my wife, Amy, and I both tested positive for Covid for the first time, but through prayer and my excellent team of doctors staying ahead of the game at UNC of Chapel Hill, NC, the symptoms were only mild.

15

Forever Thankful

BEFORE MY TRANSPLANT, while I was still at home and my health was declining, I had to be rushed to the hospital several times, usually by ambulance, but not always. I was admitted at least four times for pneumonia in one year alone and survived them all by the grace of God only.

One trip stands out in my mind from all the others. My day had started out like most did, with me slowly merging into the day from the tasks of getting up and out of bed, showering, dressing, and back to my chair, which all in all took me about three hours in the months before my actual transplant. As I was sitting in my chair adjusting my oxygen flow, I noticed that I was more out of breath than usual, so I increased my oxygen levels. It helped some, but I didn't get the relief that I got most days when I did that. In another two hours, I'd only gotten worse. My breathing had really become labored. I considered calling 911, but I procrastinated, fearing that I was overreacting a bit, so I didn't call. Plus, I'd been hospitalized so many times that I hated the sight of any hospital. Not to mention the fact that I'd been transported to the ER so many times before that I truly did not want to go again unless it was necessary. So I downplayed it.

In a matter of minutes, though, I realized I was in trouble. Big trouble! Amy called 911 and gave them all the information needed. Soon they were en route to our house to pick me up. I declined quickly before they got there, and it wasn't long before I was panic breathing. No matter how hard I tried to inhale, I couldn't get enough air into my lungs to satisfy them—and I wasn't even on my way to the hospital yet. I thought I was going to die of suffocation that day. What an awful way to go! I could only compare it to being held underwater, unable to break free, while trying to breathe through one of those tiny coffee straw/stirrers. It was terrifying, to say the least.

By the time the ambulance got there, I was rocking back and forth in my chair, unable to be still from fighting for air. I was obviously getting a little air because I was still conscious and alive, but it was such a small amount that it was of no great comfort to me at all. I remained in this condition as they loaded me on the stretcher and rolled me out of the house, down the sidewalk, and into the waiting ambulance.

I can't do this! kept running through my mind. My only consolation was that I knew the ambulance would have a BiPAP machine on board. The BiPAP forces air in and also draws it back out for the patient when they can't do it themselves. A CPAP only helps with inhaling. From my past similar episodes with this in the hospital, I'd always got relief from wearing a BiPAP, So I begged the ambulance attendants for the BiPAP. It was then that they told me that they didn't carry one. They only had a CPAP. I panicked again. How would I ever make the remainder of this trip in my condition?

They shut the doors, and we pulled out. I could see Amy close behind us through the back glass in the ambulance car as we picked up speed. I continued to rock side to side, scratching at the inside walls of the ambulance while I literally tried to cry out to God, but I couldn't, trying to get air any way I could. Next thing I knew, the attendant leaned up and told the driver something. Then the flashing red lights on top came on, and the siren kicked in as we accelerated to a high rate of speed. Amy slowly faded away through the back glass until I couldn't see her anymore.

When we arrived at the ER, I was rushed inside, and I immediately began begging the nurses and everyone I saw for a BiPAP. "Please get me a BiPAP! All I need is a BiPAP, and I'll be fine! Help me please!" I overheard a doctor standing close by say something about intubating me. I surely didn't want them to do that to me, but I knew they would if I didn't get that BiPAP and get it soon. Then it showed up. Praise God!

I then heard the disheartening words come from the nurse's mouth. "They forgot to put a part of this BiPAP back into the box!" My heart just sunk. But it was only momentarily as the next thing she said to me was, "Oh, here it is!"

I knew I was going to be okay somehow right then as I began to thank the Lord for getting me there safely and still alive. "What a good God you are," I told Him repeatedly. I grabbed the BiPAP from the nurse's hands and strapped the bulky full-face mask on. The relief was immediate and heavenly! I was glad there would be no intubating me, at least, not this time.

I learned a valuable lesson the hard way that day. I vowed right then and there not to go back home without a

BiPAP to keep in our house. And I didn't. That proved many times later to be one of the best decisions I ever made. I still have that BiPAP to this day, and after all these years, I must still use it occasionally. Anybody with these kinds of serious lung issues should have one at home. I also feel very strongly that every ambulance should be equipped with a BiPAP instead of just a CPAP.

If I were to make a list of things that need to be changed in our hospitals, I think the first rule would be that the facility must provide a separate waiting area for the patients who are immunosuppressed for any reason. I had a bad experience in an ER one night only about three to four months post-transplant. I woke up around midnight having the worst chest pains I'd ever experienced. It was 28 degrees outside and sleeting. Amy was still asleep in bed. I hated to wake her up from a peaceful sleep in a warm bed to tell her we needed to go to the ER in the middle of the night in the cold and the sleet. But I did.

As usual, she didn't complain. The hospital was only 15 minutes away, so instead of wasting time waiting for an ambulance, Amy simply helped me into the car and we headed to the hospital ER entrance. By the way, our apartment was three stories up in a building with no elevator.

Of course it was still Emory Hospital since it was mandatory that we live close to them for six months after my transplant there, so they know the huge risks that come with someone who's had a transplant more than anybody. The transplant hospitals also preach to us over and over the importance of avoiding being near sick people or germs when avoidable. Knowing this, the first thing I asked for at the ER that night was directions to the transplant recipient waiting area.

They looked at me kind of funny. "We don't have one. As a matter of fact, they don't exist."

"What?" I said. "Well, I can't sit out here with all of these sick people. It could kill me to catch even the simplest cold."

"Sorry," the ER attendant said. "This is as good as it gets, sir. You can figure out the rest."

Amy and I ended up leaving and driving back to the safety of our apartment instead of waiting at the ER. I called the on-call lung transplant coordinator, told them what had happened, and asked what I should do.

They simply said, "You're right, Mr. Norris; that's dangerous, and you did the right thing by leaving since you would have to wait and the ER was full. But I don't have an alternative for you. Should it happen again, you'll just have to risk it." He also said it's like that in all hospitals, unfortunately.

I told him it's not rocket science that a separate room should've been provided a long time ago nationwide, even worldwide. That was eight years ago, and it's still the same in that hospital today and in all hospitals, I think. Yet they've since added a new multi-story, billion-dollar tower to be used for organ transplants but not a simple waiting room for people like me.

Nothing's changed here in my hometown ER either or in any other ERs that I know of. How simple would it be to just add a separate room with separate supplied air adjacent to the existing ER waiting room? So simple! Just think of the lives that would be saved with such a simple renovation.

Transplantation is simply a trade at its best. You're trading a certain fatal illness for another condition that you'll have a better chance of surviving for a while. The lesser of two evils, if you will. Post-transplant life comes with new medicines—a lot of them too. Most of these medicines are only good for doing one thing, and that's protecting your new organ/organs from your body's immune system because it is ever trying to destroy this new and threatening thing that your body recognizes as an intruder. Your body realizes this organ is not yours and sees it as a threat to your life. It's just doing its job, but in this case, we don't want it to do too good of a job, so the anti-rejection meds are designed to weaken it. These special anti-rejection meds work great for what they're intended to do, but for the rest of your body— your organs, like the kidneys and the liver that have to process them—they may as well be poison.

I'm forever thankful and blessed that God spared my life a little longer. I'm forever indebted to my selfless donor and his family.

Amen and Amen.

God Is Good!

Yes, He Is!

Amen.

Timeline

- 12/2009 – Yearly eye exam. Optic nerve was "inflamed." I went back the following day for a retest. Testing showed the same results. Referred to an ophthalmologist.

- 01/2010 – Seen by ophthalmologist and had diagnostic imaging to rule out cystic fibrosis or any other neurological issues.

- 2/2010 – Seen by a pulmonologist, received diagnosis of IPF.

- 5/2010 – Second opinion with another pulmonologist. Same diagnosis.

- 4/2012 – Transferred to a new pulmonologist close to home.

- 7/2012 – Admitted for bronchoscopy and lung biopsy at a local hospital.

  o Oxygen order placed for in-home use when needed.

- 12/2012 – Lung biopsy performed to determine if asbestos was the cause of IPF. If positive, it would mean a different course of treatment.

- 05/2013 – First seen by the Duke transplant clinic. Continued with visits every three months until early 2014, when they did an evaluation and determined I had neuromuscular issues with right diaphragm.

- 03/2014 – Unable to walk stairs. Moved from second-floor to first-floor bedroom.

- 9/2014 – Emory Hospital, three-day evaluation for transplant

- 10/8/2014 – Emory Hospital, meeting with team/acceptance notification

- 10/9/2014 – Received first call for transplant, lungs determined not good.

- 11/24/2014 – Discharged from local hospital, treatment for breathing and possible pneumonia.

- Received second call for transplant, traveled to Emory for transplant.

- 5/14/22 – Amy and I both tested positive for Covid. Then God showed up again, and we came through it with only mild, almost unnoticeable symptoms. That's why He's God! And that's why He's our God. Amen!